The
Can-Do
Child

The
Can-Do
Child

Enriching the Everyday the Easy Way

Lorraine Allman

Foreword by Sue Atkins

Praise for The Can-Do Child

"What I love so much about this new book is its simplicity and philosophy, all set within a rigorously child-centred practice in which enjoyment is taken seriously and placed centre stage. You will love seeing your kids blossom, bloom and grow in confidence. The book is concise, clear, creative and can-do in its whole energy. It is easy to read, and if my kids weren't grown up now I'd be embracing all these super ideas and activities, naturally incorporating them into our time together."

Sue Atkins, BBC and ITV parenting expert, international parenting coach, author, broadcaster

"It's fantastic to find a book for parents that is based on a goal of helping children develop skills for a successful life, not just focussing on the here and now. With lots of fun, accessible advice, The Can-Do Child is a wonderful resource for parents who want to help their child thrive throughout childhood and into adult life."

Dr Amanda Gummer, UK's leading expert on play, play development, and child development

"Can-Do Child provides a practical and inspiring approach to enhancing your enjoyment of parenting, and relationship with your child, whilst boosting their can-do confidence and abilities. Anchored in a straightforward and insightful approach to bringing out the inner potential in your child in a way that fits really easily into everyday family life, this book will help you to help your child become happier, more independent, enterprising and resourceful. I thoroughly recommend it for both parents and professionals."

Dr. Lynne Kenney Psy.D practicing pediatric psychologist, international speaker and educator, TV host and co-author of *Bloom*, author of *5 Simple Steps To Teaching Children How They Think: Musical Thinking*

"In a world where children are increasingly measured on a narrow set of exam results, this is a book to help parents develop the skills youngsters really need in life, like resilience, resourcefulness and perseverance. Full of practical, interesting ideas, this is the essential tool kit to enable you to bring out the real potential in your child."

Tanith Carey, Author of *Taming the Tiger Parent – How to put your child's wellbeing first in a competitive world*

"I love this book and can't recommend it highly enough. Every family in the country should have one.

Time is the greatest gift we can give our children. They will be grown up before you know it and they all deserve the opportunity to have fun learning through play to problem solve and develop critical thinking skills from a very young age through toys, activities and situations.

Who knows what jobs will be out there in ten years' time? We need every child to have the confidence to accept any challenge they are faced with, and fulfil their potential as they develop into happy well-adjusted adults. I have worked with young children for fifty years and have never read a book offering so much beneficial help to parents. I love the Three Es model!

Thank you Lorraine, it is inspirational!"

Jenny Briggs, International Consultant and Early Years Trainer, creator of BenandBetty.co.uk an interactive multi-sensory learning programme for young children of all abilities

"The Can-Do Child has given me ideas for how to lead their play in a way that stimulates their creative thinking and problem solving ability. I certainly feel like it is helping them develop into confident, independent children."
M Davidson, parent

"The activities are very, very special to us as a family. They bring us together and make us actually appreciate and respect and understand each other when we're trying to solve a problem or helping each other out on a path."
Caroline H, parent

"I like how this book gives you great ideas that fit into our everyday busy lives, taking into account everyday situations and seeing an opportunity to apply the Can-Do Child methods. One of my favourite parts is where Lorraine talks about a team and family. It is so true, family is the first team your children are part of and it is important that they feel like a valued member of the team."
Trusha, parent and lifestyle blogger

"I have three children and am also a teacher of children with severe learning difficulties. I use these ideas with my own children as well as introducing them into my classroom practice, to support my students with problem solving and creative thinking. This is a practical guide, showing parents and carers how easily (and cheaply) they can enjoy their time with their child, and equip them with flexible thinking skills and can-do characteristics, which will support them to become successful adults in the modern world."

Cathy Bradshaw, parent and teacher

R∃THINK PRESS

First published in Great Britain 2017
by Rethink Press (www.rethinkpress.com)

for Dylan

CONTENTS

Note

For ease of reading and presentation, the word 'child' has been used throughout the book, but it should be substituted with 'children' where that reflects your particular situation. Similarly, the word 'parent' is used extensively, but it should be interpreted to mean anyone *in loco parentis*.

Foreword

When I first met Lorraine I was struck by her passion to explain the wider aspects of nurturing an enterprising child, to help parents and educators understand that it is something far broader than simply becoming an entrepreneur – inspiring children to be independent, free thinkers.

The idea of nurturing a Can-Do Child is what lies at the heart of this second wonderful book by Lorraine, building on her earlier work, research, and practical experiences. It is about fostering lifelong curiosity, creativity, and inventiveness. It's about helping children have a go, making mistakes and learning from these, developing an attitude and mindset of resilience, flexibility and creativity, developing good communication skills, and having the ability to work with others and the confidence to lead.

We live in a busy, frenetic, hectic world with 24/7 internet connection, an explosion of social media, and a data-driven approach to learning in schools. What I love about the Can-Do Child philosophy and all the fabulous resources Enterprising Child creates, is that it's not about having more things to do, or adding to our pressure as parents to be perfect; it's not about needing to spend more money, or indeed finding extra time.

The Three Es approach to raising a Can-Do Child is very much grounded in everyday play activities, which sadly are gradually and systematically being eroded from our children's childhood. Playing, and having fun, while learning and discovering, is hugely underestimated as a source of education and development, yet making everyday situations a place for enjoyable discovery and play is at the heart and soul of a Can-Do Child – an antidote which I warmly embrace and champion to the grade-obsessed education culture.

Putting the Can-Do Child philosophy into practice in your family will help you focus on encouraging, nurturing, sharing, playing, discovering, listening, empowering and teaching your children. It's not about being a 'pushy parent' but focused on relaxed, positive, and engaging parenting, spending quality time with your children and having fun. You will be empowering your kids with creativity, independence, tenacity, and team spirit as well as leadership and inventiveness. You'll be nurturing their self-esteem and building happy memories that will last a lifetime.

This wonderful book is bursting with simple, practical and original ideas to motivate your whole family. It shows you just how easy it is to nurture your Can-Do Child through everyday enjoyable activities. You will love seeing your kids blossom, bloom and grow in confidence in their problem solving, planning and organisational skills, as well as in all those other crucial life skills needed for when they step out into the big wide world of work.

What I love so much about this new book is its simplicity and philosophy, all set within a rigorously child-centred practice in which enjoyment is taken seriously and placed centre stage. This reminds me of one of my favourite quotes:

"Play is often talked about as if it were a relief from serious learning. But for children, play is serious learning."

Fred Rogers

I love the fact that this book is not about 'fixing' everything for our kids but empowering them to find solutions rather than focusing on problems. It's about building what I call the 'We Team' of being a family, and having fun spending TIME together. Real life examples combined with great activities such as 'Top Dog' (a fun way to teach responsibility) encourage kids to set goals for themselves that will give them something to aim for and focus on, because that teaches them to motivate and inspire themselves!

I really love that children will learn that they *can* make a difference in the world.

This book is concise, clear, creative and can-do in its whole energy. It is easy to read, and if my kids weren't grown up now I'd be embracing all these super ideas and activities, naturally incorporating them into our time together.

How exciting to think that by simply having fun with your children and exploring the ideas in this book you can be developing a creative, innovative, independent, resourceful, and resilient child using Can-Do Child's core values of Engagement, Enterprise, and Enjoyment.

What better gift can you give your children?

Sue Atkins
BBC and ITV parenting expert, international parenting coach, author, and broadcaster

Why The Can-Do Child

Parenting and educating children amounts to one of the biggest challenges we will ever face in our lives. We feel an enormous responsibility for bringing up a child, helping them to discover their passion and talents, and developing in them the inner resources to face life's challenges and to make the most of opportunities. One of the greatest gifts we can give to our children is to nurture in them the character traits and skills that will help them to be creative and innovative, independent and resilient; to play and work well with others; to make sound judgements; and to have a justified self-confidence in their own abilities and perceptions. This is what I mean when I speak of a Can-Do Child. This book is for you if you want an effective and easy-to-use guide to raising a Can-Do Child.

The role of parents and carers is crucial in character formation and in the emotional and intellectual development of children. Focusing my research on the extent of their influence, resulted in the publication of *Enterprising Child* in 2012.

The book proved popular, particularly among parents who were already running their own businesses, and it acted as a very practical guide to nurturing enterprising characteristics through play. However, it left the problem of how to explain in simple terms to those who hadn't read the book that being 'enterprising' meant something much more fundamental than being 'an entrepreneur'. I looked again at how to foster an understanding that this was not about creating mini business people, but about nurturing a set of core characteristics, skills and attitude – a mindset relevant not just to the world of work and business in adult years, but also to the experience of childhood exploration and play, and to all forms of learning and life in general. It is with this in mind that this second book has been written, and entitled *The Can-Do Child*.

Whilst there are many books on parenting techniques and ways to 'manage' children, there is very little support, if any, given to help parents learn how to bring out the best in their child's can-do nature. This encourages parents to nurture those fundamental characteristics from a young age, using a tried and tested play based approach endorsed by top child psychologists, early years, and parenting experts.

The underpinning can-do philosophy is covered in more detail in the next chapter, which looks at the three core elements of raising a Can-Do Child, but it is clear from talking with parents, and others working in the fields of parenting, child play, and child psychology, that there is a growing appreciation of the benefit of helping children to become more self-managing, adventurous, innovative, and resourceful. Whilst I believe that children are naturally enterprising – curious, inventive, imaginative, and remarkably resilient and determined, as all parents will know – there are also cultural and educational factors in our risk-averse, grade-obsessed society that are stifling children and indeed parent's natural can-do nature and confidence.

Why Now?

There are two reasons why I believe this book is particularly timely. The first of these relates to the impact of socio-economic and technological change upon the future prospects of our children. The second is much more to do with problems affecting the quality of family life in the here and now. So let's start with that.

Creating a Better Now

Research has shown that parents of children,[1] as well as children themselves,[2] are becoming increasingly stressed, so clearly, as a society, we are not doing well on both counts. A happy family life for both parent and child is essential for the child's healthy development, but it is also something we would all want for our families as a good in itself. The philosophy and approach explained in this book, focused on making the most of your relationship with your child, encouraging their zest for life, and maximising enjoyment for both parent and child, are an important way for parents, no matter how

---

1 www.nytimes.com/2015/11/05/upshot/stressed-tired-rsuhed-a-portrait-of-the-modern-family.html

2 www.bbc.co.uk/news/education-3594008 April 2016

time- or resource-poor, to boost the quality and enjoyableness of family life.

Creating a Better Future

The job market is different now from what it was even ten years ago, and our children need to be prepared for a future in which the impact of technological and global economic change on employment patterns will place far more emphasis upon the need for individuals to recognise, and indeed create, opportunities for themselves, rather than slotting into established jobs for life.

When Enterprising Child was written in 2012 I discussed the issues raised by employers who had jobs to offer but complained of the lack of 'work readiness' among school leavers – citing in particular a lack of initiative, poor self-management, and little ability to work with others – a trend some feel continues to be reinforced by a tightly prescribed educational curriculum focused on maximising individual academic results, leaving little scope for exploration away from the beaten tracks of exam-ready knowledge.

It is with sadness, but no great surprise, that research indicates very little has changed over the last four years with employers continuing to raise concerns about the lack of preparation for school leavers in areas such as self-management, team working, and communication skills.[3] In one major workforce survey[4] 88% of businesses believe school leavers are unprepared for the workplace, with many lacking 'soft skills' such as communication, team working, and resilience. A staggering 92% of employers in one survey said they are experiencing skills shortages in areas such as problem solving, planning and organisational skills.

These figures are not unique to the UK as the UNESCO report[4] on Skills Gaps across the world, covering Africa, Asia, Europe, North America and more, demonstrates.

3 http://news.cbi.org.uk/reports/education-and-skills-survey-2015/
4 http://unesdoc.unesco.org/images/0021/002178/217874e.pdf

So, factors such as globalisation, economic liberalism and the development of AI and robotics all have a serious structural effect upon future job markets and patterns of work. There are other factors too, such as de-industrialisation and the rise of a service and knowledge based economy, which also impact upon the need for the next generation to have far better personal learning skills, interpersonal skills, adaptability, and resourcefulness than previous generations may have required – resulting in a developing skills gap in the area of 'soft skills'. All of which makes this book particularity timely as we consider the need to raise a can-do generation who can adapt, survive, and flourish in a future that is already unfolding around us.

As parents and educators, we may not be able to do much about the macroeconomic factors affecting our children's future, but we can help to nurture in them the attitudes and skills they will need to become active participants rather than bystanders in the unfolding of that future. This is surely the least we owe to them, enabling them to take control of their lives and make a difference.

What is this book about?

This book is all about how to nurture a can-do attitude and skill set in your child through everyday moments and occasional planned activities using the easy to remember Three Es approach focusing on:

- Parental Engagement
- Enterprising activities
- Enjoyment

A can-do attitude covers a multitude of skills and abilities, including creative thinking and doing, problem solving, working well with others, communication skills, managing risk and developing resilience, inventiveness, ambition, understanding and appreciating others and their needs, and working to improve things for everyone not just one's self.

This book is about what you do with the time you have with your child. It is not about having more things to do, needing to spend more money, or indeed finding extra time. The Three Es approach to raising a Can-Do Child is very much grounded in everyday play activity, often hugely underestimated as a source of learning and development in our culture, and making everyday situations and tasks a context for enjoyable discovery and play.

© Phil Adams

"Creativity is easily encouraged and can be taught (in children) through everyday parenting, not just through painting and model-making, but through play in general and how they learn to channel creativity and develop their view of the world."

Paul Lindley, founder of Ella's Kitchen, Paddys' Bathroom, and Dad to Ella and Paddy

The Philosophy of the Can-Do Child

The philosophy underpinning the nurturing of a Can-Do Child has been developed following more than 15 years of research and practical work with young people, and is supported by top parenting, child development, and early years experts. It helps parents and educators nurture in children the characteristics, skills, and innovative behaviours necessary to succeed in a world that has changed dramatically from the last century.

Each aspect of the can-do philosophy is supported with insight and understanding collected from extensive interviews, research, and years of practical experience in the fields of enterprise, education, child psychology, and parenting.

A formal definition of success is not offered, as each person and each culture may have differing definitions as to what counts as success, however the primary focus is on supporting our children now, and as they grow older, to be happy, creative, and confident, and to find fulfilment in adding value to the world in some way that benefits others as well as themselves, making the best use of their talents and opportunities.

What will you get from this book?

This book provides an easy, fun, tried and tested approach to nurturing happy, creative, confident children with a can-do approach to life, ready to be the best they can. It is suitable for parents, grandparents, childminders, educators, in fact anyone *in loco parentis* or who has an interest in this important work.

Here are some of the things I hope you will take away with you:

- An understanding of the Three Es approach developed through years of research and practical experience, backed by top parenting, child development, and early years experts. This is a universally applicable, non-prescriptive, flexible model which allows you to adapt its implementation for your own family culture or circumstances.

- How to use everyday situations and simple activities to nurture key character traits and skills in your child, keep them busy, and have great family fun!

- A play based approach you can feel confident in which enables you to help your child be the best they can without compromising any aspect of their childhood.

The primary focus is on supporting our children now, and as they grow older, to be happy, creative, and confident. This book is not intended as a complete parenting manual, and does not focus on the everyday trials and tribulations of raising children, although you are likely to find the approach and sample activities may well come in handy to minimise the impact of these. I am also confident that using the Three Es to raise your Can-Do Child will strengthen your bond with them still further, with a positive impact on other areas of family life.

"As a family, the approach and activities are very, very special. They bring us together and make us actually appreciate, respect and understand each other when you're trying to solve a problem or helping each other out on a path."

Caroline H, parent

Why should you, as a parent or educator, read this book?

We are often deluged with messages from books, magazines, and the media about how to achieve success in raising children in whatever way a particular model determines, for example producing more obedient/more successful/busier children (delete as applicable).

I am not interested in peddling a particular definition of success, or putting greater pressure on us to try and fit children into some preconceived mould. My goal is simply to help; because as a parent myself I know that you, the most significant person in your child's life, are the person best equipped to help them be themselves and achieve their full potential.

The importance of character

"'Character' can help boost educational attainment and motivation to learn among young people, as well as facilitating positive later life outcomes, such as good mental well-being, positive health behaviours, and more success in the labour market."

Character Nation, Demos 2015, Jonathan Birdwell, Ralph Scott, Louis Reynolds[5]

This quote is taken directly from a report which draws on research into character produced by the Jubilee Centre for Character and Virtues at the University of Birmingham, as well as studies into different attributes of character that are referred to as 'soft skills', 'social and emotional skills' and 'non-cognitive skills'. Referring to research carried out by the Early Intervention Foundation (EIF) the report tells us:

"Self-control and self-regulation in childhood were associated with various aspects of adult life, including 'mental health, life satisfaction and well-being, income and labour market outcomes, measures of physical health, obesity, smoking, crime and mortality.'

5 www.demos.co.uk/project/demos-character-programme/

"Good or healthy self-perceptions and self-awareness... in childhood were associated with positive later life results relating to 'mental distress, self-rated health, obesity and unemployment'."

The Demos report is concerned specifically with the education sector, looking at how 'character development' can best be incorporated into schools, and the case for doing so, but it is clear that when it comes to character development the influence of parents is enormous.

Feedback from parents tells us that the enterprising can-do philosophy and activities are perfect for developing characteristics such as self-reliance, conscientiousness, social skills, self-regulation, motivation and determination. The research above shows us how crucial these are to success and happiness in adult years.

We know children are designed to learn and grow, and that they do this best by doing what comes naturally – by playing and having fun. It's essential that family life is based on mutual enjoyment and a growing appreciation of one another. It is the organic process of character development that comes from encouragement and loving support given to children that is the key to all other good things—whatever particular outcome we are focusing upon such as material, emotional, social or indeed 'spiritual' success in life. The following chapters will show you just how easy it is to achieve these great outcomes, and make your family life more enjoyable in the process simply by doing the things that come naturally.

Understanding the importance of positive character development, and using the Three Es approach introduced in this book will help children develop the following character traits:

Character Traits
of the Can-Do Child

Creative and Innovative

Independent / Self-Reliance

Imaginative

Resourceful

Resilience

Sound Judgements / Decision-Making

Self-Confidence

Adventurous

Curiosity

Social Skills

Ambition

Self-Regulation

Determination

Play and work well with others

Social Awareness

Critical Thinking

Problem Solving

Planning and Organisation

While most of these character traits are fairly self-explanatory, I wanted to take a few moments to look at three in particular:

- Social Skills
- Self-Regulation
- Social Awareness

Social Skills

Social Skills is a phrase which encompasses the multitude of skills needed to help us in relationships of all kinds. This includes the way in which we communicate and interpret speech and behaviour of others, both verbal and non-verbal, how we present ourselves and interact with others, and our ability to socialise and build relationships. In childhood, one example among many is the ability to 'take turns' in conversation, showing interest in what the other person is saying and not constantly interrupting or ignoring what they are trying to communicate.

Self-Regulation

Self-regulation is necessary to enable us to monitor and control our behaviour, emotions, and thoughts depending on the situations we find ourselves in.

In parenting children, we seek to help them move from functioning within the external framework provided for them to regulate their behaviour, to one where they demonstrate effective self-regulation. At an early age it is often necessary to physically prevent children from impulsively engaging in activities that may threaten their physical safety or infringe the rights of others, but the longer term goal is always to help them achieve an internal capacity to manage their own behaviour. In this way, children develop a sense of patience and persistence, learning that it can pay to defer instant pleasures for a greater reward, and that success will usually depend upon continued effort, not giving up if things don't work out immediately. Self-regulation is also essential for moral behaviour, and that is an important feature of turning *social awareness* into positive, value based choices and actions.

Social Awareness

Social Awareness begins where there is *engagement* between parent and child. It is here the child first gains a sense of self, and of the 'otherness' of those around them. Social Awareness introduces the notion of value, and the ability to see one's self as part of a social system in which there are compromises to be made in the interest of mutual benefit, quite often through foregoing immediate demands for individual gratification. As a child's social awareness increases so their awareness of the needs of others and the ability to gain satisfaction from giving as well as receiving grows too. These foundational experiences can then be mapped onto a widening experience of a sense of community and mutual interests and obligations – first within the extended family, later in the wider community, through to conceptions of civil responsibility and duty, along with a broadening circle of altruistic concern, and a sense of global interconnection.

ELEMENTS

The Three Es
of a Can-Do Child

The three elements – Engagement, Enterprise and Enjoyment – are crucial to the nurturing of your Can-Do Child. Each element is covered in more detail and its importance explained in separate chapters, but very briefly these crucial building blocks are defined on the next page:

Engagement refers to the dynamic relationship of support, trust, and encouragement parents establish with their children from the very earliest age.

Enterprise is the child's attitude of initiative, resourcefulness, and resilience. It is one of the key characteristics underlying children's learning, and parental engagement is crucial in providing an enabling framework for this.

Enjoyment may seem self-explanatory but it is surprisingly often overlooked that children's development and learning is fuelled by enjoyment, providing a motivating energy for ongoing exploration, discovery, and learning for children and adults alike.

ELEMENT ONE
ENGAGEMENT

"We're building a house at the moment and Iolo loves getting involved. He has his own toolbox and helps out with small jobs like moving timber and clearing up after a job is done. I think it's good that he sees me doing lots of things in and around the house and garden, so it's natural for him to want to help."

Ben, Dad to Iolo (6) and Rufus (2½)

This chapter will help you:

- Understand the role of engagement in nurturing your Can-Do Child

- Feel confident in identifying ways to increase the quality of your engagement with your child

- Learn practical ways to nurture can-do characteristics in your child

Definition

"Positive parent-child relationships provide the foundation for children's learning. With parents' sensitive, responsive, and predictable care, young children develop the skills they need to succeed in life. Early parent-child relationships have powerful effects on children's emotional well-being (Dawson & Ashman, 2000), their basic coping and problem-solving abilities, and future capacity for relationships."(Lerner & Castellino, 2002)

All human learning and development takes place within a social context where the quality of adult-child and child-child relationships are hugely important in facilitating that learning and development.

Engagement is simply the relationship of support, trust, and encouragement parents establish with their children. Through this relationship, and through play, your child is learning to engage and interact in the world around them, and this is why engagement is one of the key elements to raising a Can-Do Child.

Role Model

One of the most crucial aspects of engagement with your child is role modelling. Long before children acquire the ability to process language and understand instructions they are learning by watching and internalising what they see. This is particularly so in the formative early years, so as parents we have a very important part to play in this respect.

Modelling positive traits such as curiosity and perseverance, listening to the ideas of others, and taking a methodical approach to problems can have a powerfully beneficial effect on our children. We don't have to be perfect – in fact it is better to demonstrate openness about our mistakes coupled with a sense of curiosity and determination in the resolution of problems. Involving children, where appropriate, to help find solutions to problems, encouraging them to explore and find things out for themselves is an important part of their development.

Children are learning from us all the time how things are done, whether that's something practical or physical such as mixing colours, jumping up and down, or expressing emotions such as happiness or frustration.

Team Family

> *"As a family, the approach and activities are very, very special. They bring us together and make us actually appreciate, respect and understand each other when you're trying to solve a problem or helping each other out on a path."*
>
> **Caroline H, parent**

Whether your family is large or small, home provides a perfect setting for your child to learn and explore what it means to be part of a team, to engage with one another, in a supportive setting.

Accomplishing tasks together reinforces teamwork and the value of working together towards one common goal. The family is the first team your child is a member of, and what they learn in the home team will shape their attitudes and character for years to come.

Developing your child's understanding of, and capacity to, work within or lead a team will help develop valuable communication skills, including how to negotiate and motivate. This will involve building confidence in their judgements, but also a respect for facts and the importance of thinking things through in decision making.

The ability to engage with others in effective communication is an essential ingredient in enabling your child's resourcefulness to make a real difference in the world. When they are able to express their ideas and passions clearly, they can engage others in their enthusiasm.

Encourage your child to express themselves, to listen, and to exchange ideas and develop the art of open communication.

How to Engage

"I let my four-year old completely plan our family Boxing Day from deciding the menu to sorting out games and even the dress code. I was amazed with her ideas and her ability to plan and make lists (she sees me making to-do lists all the time!). I now take the time to explain to her what I am doing with my work and why, trying to get her involved with little tasks like taking pictures for the blog."

Trusha, Mum and blogger at SecretStyleFile.com

We all know that sometimes trying to engage with our child is not as easy as it sounds, and keeping their interest when they have a more limited attention span than adults can be a real challenge, but if you can connect with what your child enjoys (enjoyment is the third 'e' of raising a Can-Do Child – more about that later), you are likely to find this greatly rewarding in terms of the impact it has upon your child's enjoyment of their time with you, and vice-a-versa, as well as knowing you are providing a crucial ingredient for their personal development.

The trick is to avoid applying adult filters to your experience; the things that interest your child may not seem terribly fascinating to you – we all know that young children love repetition, apparently *ad nauseam* – but understanding that through childish interests and enthusiasms there is a deeper and innate process of learning going on should help avoid the trap of always trying to move things along rather than staying in the moment with your child and feeling their enjoyment and excitement in the here and now.

Principles

As you engage with your child in playful activities it is also useful to bear in mind the following:

Share Enthusiasm

Sharing your enthusiasm can be infectious; children need to learn to identify, accept, and feel approval for their enjoyment in playful activity and learning. By communicating enthusiasm you connect with their world and help them connect with themselves as well as you.

Let Them Lead

Give your child the opportunity to lead in an activity or at the very least ensure they have an active role. Depending on the activity it could be simply acting out parts of a story or taking the appropriate items out of the fridge ready for baking.

Real-Life Experiences

Providing real-life hands on experiences will really benefit your child – screen based time playing games has its value, but real-life activities have the advantage of allowing for richer human to human interaction.

Ask Questions
Look at the importance of conversation in engagement, especially asking questions. Talking with children about their experiences helps them make sense of the world and their experience of it as they explore and experiment.

Mirroring
Summarising your child's communications to you is a very powerful way to show them that you are engaged with them. It also helps them develop greater awareness. This can be non-verbal – if your child is excited or happy its best to communicate your own happiness or excitement, matching your non-verbal signals to your content ("that's lovely" said in a bored tone of voice tends to create a sense of confusion and insecurity in children just as much as in adults). It can also be verbal, so paraphrasing back to your child the content of their communications helps them know that you have heard what they

have said, feel understood, and also helps them identify, own, and manage their feelings, be they positive or negative.

Some of the above may seem a little daunting to over stretched parents, however it is important to remember that perfection is not required – doing what comes naturally and being 'good enough' will do. In fact not always getting things right, and showing how you handle that, is an important part of the process as it also introduces the idea of reparation and repair, which is a crucial ingredient in understanding relationships. Whilst I would never encourage any parent to fail to show empathy or to snap at their child because they are too busy to look at something that is important to the child, these things do happen as I know all too well, so the key is to understand the learning which presents itself from this lapse in parental perfection. Apologising for our understandable lapses into self-preoccupation is a valuable learning experience for children because it tells them that we can all fail, but that relationships based on love show the possibility of things being mended by honesty and an apology.

The Three Es approach is inherently activity based and as will be shown later, it is in everyday interactive activities that the three elements perform their magic. Further guidance and examples follow shortly to show how simple yet powerfully beneficial everyday, or easily planned activities can be woven into the fabric of everyday family life.

Summary

To fully engage with your child in a way that nurtures their can-do character traits it is essential to be actively involved in their lives by:

- Providing a secure base from which they can develop their independence

- Providing appropriate role modelling

- Entering their world and positively reinforcing their play based learning by communicating acceptance and enthusiasm

- Helping them to interpret and learn from their experiences by asking questions and providing supportive mirroring

ELEMENT TWO
ENTERPRISE

"You teach your children all sorts of mindsets and attitudes. If you're creating an enterprising attitude in your home, not a pushy entrepreneurial one about money at all costs, but that mindset of communication, team working, critical thinking, thinking outside the box and being creative, and using your initiative, what better place to start than at home?"

Sue Atkins, BBC and ITV parenting expert, international author and broadcaster

This chapter will help you:

- Understand what is meant by enterprise and an enterprising mindset

- Understand why enterprise is so crucial to raising a Can-Do Child

- Learn practical ways to nurture enterprising characteristics in your child

Definition

Enterprising,[6] adjective (definition): Having or showing initiative and resourcefulness.

Enterprising[7] (synonyms):resourceful,imaginative, ingenious, inventive, original, creative, quick-witted, bright, sharp, talented, capable, spirited, enthusiastic, dynamic, ambitious, energetic, courageous, intrepid, adventurous.

It is clear that being enterprising, as defined above, is an essential characteristic of a Can-Do Child. An enterprising mindset is relevant not just to the world of work in adult years, but also to the experience of childhood exploration and play, and to all forms of learning and life in general. This is why enterprise is one of the three core elements of raising a Can-Do Child.

Parents Role

As parents, we do a vital job in supporting children with their learning: in numeracy not just by teaching them how to count, but helping them solve problems and think logically; in literacy

6 www.oxforddictionaries.com/definition/english/enterprising

7 www.collinsdictionary.com/dictionary/english-thesaurus/enterprising

by helping them develop good communication skills – listening and talking has a direct bearing on a child's ability to read and write; and encouraging learning about themselves and the world around them through play, developing cognitive concepts (what does this do/what will happen next?), and important social skills (how to co-operate, negotiate, take turns). In all of this, we are already having a direct impact on our children's educational, emotional and social development – not to mention their confidence.

We also, however, have a crucial role in supporting and encouraging our children to make the best of themselves, to work towards fulfilling their full potential, and to be able to navigate the complexities of a rapidly changing world. It is in this respect that nurturing enterprise has such an important part to play. We know that in the formation of character and attitudes, which are the foundation for acquiring appropriate practical skills and knowledge, the parent's role, from the earliest of years before formal education has even begun, is absolutely crucial.

The Inventive Side of Play

"...there is a definite connection between the playfulness required for invention and the inventive side of play. Inventiveness...is a set of mental and hands-on skills such as creative and critical thinking, problem-solving, flexibility, risk-taking, collaboration, and communication. Successful inventors often credit their parents for providing the environment and encouragement to develop those habits and while there are no clear set of traits all inventors share, there are qualities they share such as curiosity, persistence, imagination, and improvisation which are the cornerstones of the inventor's toolkit."

Monica M. Smith, Head of Exhibitions and Interpretation, Smithsonian's Lemelson Center for the Study of Invention and Innovation at the National Museum of American History

Things Not Working Out

It is important your child is supported in becoming comfortable with things not working as expected. Sometimes successful inventions, and scientific discoveries, come about because of that serendipity moment when there is an unexpected event. Often it is just in the nature of the process of inventing that an initially promising route appears to be a dead end, or it is necessary to 'go back to the drawing board' and start again.

If your child can learn to cope with the frustrations this may cause, even to relish the challenge and the need to be flexible and responsive to the information their activities are providing them with, then they will benefit greatly.

It's OK to Make Mistakes

Children are far more likely to develop their can-do approach to life with a resourceful, resilient attitude, where they are given opportunities to explore and experiment and receive positive support, even when things don't quite work out as expected. Nothing impedes creativity and innovation more than the fear of getting things wrong, the idea that there is a "right" way to do things, and if you don't get it right, then somehow you have failed. In our constantly monitored, assessed, and graded educational system it is all too easy to succumb to the pressure to ensure all children learn the approved answers to set questions likely to come up in assessments and exams, and to use only the 'approved' methods to demonstrate their workings. This can create a crippling fear of making mistakes in children, particularly so in those who have grown used to succeeding and so become more fearful of failing, impeding learning and creativity.

If children are to overcome a fear of failure it is crucial to convey that "failure is feedback" an essential and inherently valuable part of the process of discovery and creativity. It is not something to be feared, rather embraced and recognised for the benefits it brings. Modelling this to our children through our own behaviour at home is important. A simple example of this is if the toast burns or the eggs are too hard boiled – involve your child in a light hearted discussion about what happened and why, demonstrating that mistakes are not disasters but opportunities to learn more about cause and effect and to find better ways to do things.

Can We Fix It?

"Problem solving for me as a parent is one of my biggest fears, of them losing that. The first reaction is to call home if something goes wrong, but through the [Can-Do Child] activities they will realise they can sort it out for themselves, come up with solutions for problems."

Beatriz N, parent

It's natural for us parents to want to 'fix' things for our children when things go wrong, but giving them the opportunities to work out solutions for themselves will not only build their confidence and self-belief, it will also develop their imaginative and independent thinking skills as they mature. Children learn problem solving skills best through experiences which are meaningful to them and in the everyday, so finding the 'teachable moments', creating space for your child to explore and experiment with solutions to problems rather than hurrying them through to a resolution that depends upon your intervention, is to be encouraged.

At a young age, children can easily become frustrated, so do offer help if you feel that will head off a meltdown. As they mature, children are cognitively more able to imagine and think through problems and potential solutions with less hands-on experience. Encouraging your child to focus less on the problem and more on finding a solution develops their creative thinking abilities as well as problem-solving skills. Involvement in family decisions and problem solving, praising their efforts to reason through different scenarios, and modelling how we as parents work through possible solutions to problems will all help our children learn to undertake that process themselves.

Risk and Resilience

It is important for children to learn not just resilience and perseverance, but also the delicate balance between tenacity and courage in the face of adversity, the wisdom to know when they need to keep going, when to stop and, if necessary, think again. If risk awareness is nurtured without resilience then a child is likely to be afraid to ever venture beyond their comfort zone. However a Spartan-like focus on resilience without an awareness of risk will result in recklessness and an inability or unwillingness to know when to reassess the wisdom of any course of action.

As children grow up, they need increasing independence to make their own decisions and must learn to manage risk and take responsibility for their actions. One of the most important aspects of being able to make decisions is self-confidence. If they are confident in their ability to analyse a situation, they will feel confident enough to make the right decision.

As a parent, you can help your child develop confidence, experience, and judgement by being prepared to let go and allowing them to make age-appropriate decisions. Your child needs confidence in their own ability to act appropriately, as well as in line with their personal values.

As with any situation where there is risk of failure, it is important they (and you) view this as an opportunity for learning – to pick themselves up, reflect and move on, to show resilience or 'bounce back'. Encourage your child to become confident in making well informed decisions, and to be someone not content to simply follow the crowd or reliant upon others to tell them what to do. By providing opportunities for your child to identify and manage risk, and take responsibility for their own actions, you are helping your child grow in confidence, wisdom, and the courage to create.

"I like to sit and explain reasons why we have to do certain things with my children, especially Sophie, rather than coming out with the usual rushed 'because I said so'. Sophie at four is really starting to understand things better now and we can talk about decisions concerning money. For example, the other day she wanted to go on a bouncy castle but I had already planned for us to visit the Science Centre. We discussed the options and the money involved and she decided she'd stick with the Science Centre."

Cheryl Ryder, mum to Sophie (4), Craig (2½), Callum (1½)

Seeing the Bigger Picture

In a world often preoccupied with commercial gain it would be easy to overlook the fact that there is a moral and social framework within which children need to be educated; helping them understand that the world is not equal in terms of access to shelter, healthcare, finance, education, environment, and much more, introduces them to the moral and social impact of human activity. They also need to learn they can make a difference and that putting in effort to help others can bring a great sense of reward. This core realisation will stay with children as they grow and develop, and provide an ongoing incentive to realising value and overcoming obstacles with compassion and a creative approach to social problems, a cornerstone of their can-do character.

Giving something back to society whether by volunteering, solving problems through innovation, fundraising, or donating money, means recognising the value inherent in all human life, the earth and all its creatures. It means acknowledging that our own gifts carry responsibilities and that we are not here just to pursue our private wellbeing.

As your child matures they can be introduced to practical examples of how to 'give back' to society and make a positive contribution to the welfare of others. They can learn how it is possible, in spite of their young age, to either have a say in, or even take action on, the things that they care deeply about, through exploring with them in an age appropriate way local and global social issues, and inspiring in them the desire to do more.

Setting Goals

All children like to get involved in activities, to be 'hands on' and this needs to be matched in us as parents by encouraging a can-do attitude, trying out new ideas as many times as necessary to achieve the desired result, harnessing their ambition to do things better.

A child's willingness to experiment and take risks, combined with their inherent ambition means they will want to achieve and take opportunities to be creative, often not being content with the status quo.

I positively encourage you to encourage your child to 'dream' – have a picture of the moon they want one day to walk on, or of the mountain they want to climb, or of a person they would one day like to emulate. The thing to encourage at this stage is ambition – the key to which is the motivating energy, rather than the final goal itself. Whether they reach that goal or not, instilling an ambitious rather than defeatist approach to life will really help develop your child's can-do character.

Formulating a goal, imagining what it will look or feel like to achieve that goal, making it tangible and specific, helps in the act of working towards that goal. It provides both motivation and the means to identify necessary steps or sub-goals. It will also encourage your child to look forward, to aspire and make it more likely they will succeed.

As a parent you can help your child set goals that are both achievable but which are also stretching so they receive the positive reinforcement of having achieved something which was a challenge that they both accepted and met.

Principles

Provide a secure base

Children are emboldened to explore and experiment when they have a secure attachment figure (that means you) that they can return to for acceptance and a sense of safety and security. Children do not learn by being thrown in at the deep end and feeling abandoned, they learn to be independent by, in the first instance and as they progress, always having a safe person to whom they can return as they gradually venture further afield, both literally and metaphorically.

Avoid Pressure to 'succeed'

Avoid any pressure upon your child to perform to a particular standard or to 'succeed'. Mistakes are to be welcomed. A child who is afraid to make mistakes will become afraid to try or learn new things, since all learning almost inevitably involves an initial period of struggling before mastery is achieved. Appreciate their efforts with a balance of praise, and words of encouragement to try again and/or improve.

Don't rush to fix things

It's tempting to step in and help your child find the solution to a problem a little quicker than they may on their own, but taking a step back can reap rewards in terms of your child developing confidence in their problem solving abilities. Give them opportunities and time to explore, experiment, be involved in discussions and decisions, and remember to model how you solve problems too.

Use their natural talents and interests for good

Encourage your child to use their natural skills and talents to benefit others. This could be something as straightforward as getting involved in a sponsored run or bake if they enjoy running or cooking, to something more elaborate such as volunteering at an animal shelter if they have a particular interest and care for animals.

The key is to ensure that they are learning that they can make a difference in the world, and recognise their wider role in society.

Summary

- Enterprise is about showing initiative and resourcefulness. It is an essential ingredient for a Can-Do Child.

- Being enterprising is itself a character trait, but for it to be fully realised it requires the development of important skills such as communication, interpersonal, and problem solving, as well as the cultivation of related traits such as curiosity, imagination, resilience and tenacity.

- The formative influence of parents, through appropriate engagement and the celebration of enjoyment in innovation and discovery, is central in developing enterprise, and the can-do character traits and skill sets, in children.

- Find the 'teachable moments' in the everyday by creating space for your child to explore and experiment with solutions to problems, to innovate, set goals, learn how to work together rather than in isolation, to make mistakes and learn from those, to develop sufficient self-confidence to 'bounce back', and to consider others will go a very long way to nurturing enterprise in your Can-Do Child.

ENJOYMENT ENTERPRISE

THE CAN-DO CHILD

ENGAGEMENT

ELEMENT THREE
ENJOYMENT

"Play is a fantastic way to promote family cohesion, enhance child development, reduce stress and encourage parents and children to enjoy their family life."

Dr Amanda Gummer, child development expert and play psychologist

This chapter will help you understand:

- How you and your child can better enjoy your time together

- The value of play and enjoyment for both adult and child

- The importance of enjoyment in nurturing a can-do approach to life

Definition

All learning starts with play, and the capacity to be playful is a great way to facilitate learning, in ourselves as well as in our children. As adults it is essential we retain our capacity for play in order, as Dr Gummer says, to help us enjoy family life. Enjoyment is the very essence of play, however, before I expand on this I want to be clear why 'enjoyment' was specifically chosen over 'excitement' as the third element of the can-do philosophy.

The Pressure to be Exciting

I considered 'excitement' for some time as it seemed to be a more fun, energising kind of word. The difficulty I had with it, speaking very much with my parent hat on, is that frankly not everything we do with our children is or can be exciting. There is a lot of pressure on parents, particularly those working full-time to make sure that when we do get to spend time with our children it has to be fun and exciting. That can be a tall order when you've just got in from work, have a meal to prepare, and there's homework to be done.

On top of that, there seems to be considerably less time for children to experience 'free play' these days[8] and the existence of a more generally 'hurried' family life with recent research showing families on an average day are spending just 38 minutes together.[9] In fact enjoyment doesn't necessarily have to involve obvious play at all – just sitting companionably can be enjoyable, or running a stick along the ground as you walk; we don't always need to be looking actively for the 'learning' in play as in life, sometimes just giving your child space to enjoy being in the world is the most important thing we can do.

"...Children need to have stand-and-stare time, time imagining and pursuing their own thinking processes or assimilating their experiences through play or just observing the world around them...It is this sort of thing that stimulates the imagination."

Dr Teresa Belton, Visiting Fellow in the School of Education and Lifelong learning, University of East Anglia

Focusing on enjoyment rather than excitement feels more manageable, balanced, and realistic.

8 www.express.co.uk/news/uk/654424/Children-now-spending-less-time-out-side-than-PRISONERS

9 www.netmums.com/activities/free-family-fun/families-spend-less-than-40-minutes-a-day-together

Of course, I hope that there are plenty of times when excitement is evident – children enjoy excitement and fun, love to laugh and experience thrills and be a bit wild, this is an important ingredient in childhood no matter how exhausting parents and grandparents find it at times. Equally, however, your child will not learn to appreciate life's gentler pleasures if they are constantly being subjected to only highly stimulating forms of activity, potentially growing into adults who constantly crave high adrenaline thrills to be happy.

"Evidence from anthropological, psychological, neuroscientific and educational studies have identified play as an adaptation that enabled early humans to become powerful learners and problem-solvers."

New Scientist

However you play with your child, and that will vary depending on your own family circumstances and their particular needs, ensuring enjoyment is at the centre of it is key for their cognitive, social, physical, and emotional well-being. It enables your child to develop that positive can-do mindset in so many ways. For example, following your child's lead rather than directing the play will help them (and you) discover what interests them, the pace at which they learn, and provide opportunities to practice their decision making skills, to be creative, and perhaps innovate.

Parenting in the Here and Now

I mentioned at the start the importance for us as adults to retain our capacity for play. We have a lot to worry about these days, but in order to experience enjoyment in play time with our children it is necessary to be in the present with them, rather than worrying about things we have or haven't done, or even the mess that's going to have to be cleared up after an activity is over. Joining your child on this level is not only essential to ensuring a real sense of engagement, as opposed to perhaps a little distracted co-presence, but also introduces a therapeutic element of mindfulness into your life as adult preoccupations are put aside and you enter into the eternal *now* of child-like absorption in the serious business of play.

Everyday Moments

Some of the greatest enjoyment between parent and child happens in the 'everyday' and this is actually some of the best quality time you can spend with them. By 'everyday' I mean having a conversation about where you are or what you're doing (perhaps driving along in the car, walking to the park, or even stuck in a queue), when you're preparing the family dinner together, doing some gardening, on a bike ride, or simply on your hands and knees building Lego® or making up a game.

"The most noticeable change has been in my 5 year-old. He is much quieter and more introverted than his brother, but activities like encouraging him to join in and build on the stories we read together, and asking him why he thinks certain day-to-day things happen have really brought him out of his shell, with often hilarious results."

M Davidson, Dad to 9 year old and 5 year old

Principles
Follow your Child's Lead
Notice what they enjoy, deepen their sense of enjoyment and stimulate their exploration by mirroring and amplifying their experience with favourable comments and questions.

Noticing the Spark
A Can-Do Child will take enjoyment in their capacity to problem solve, create, innovate, and persevere, however they will only find this if their formative experiences of experimenting, learning, and creating are inherently enjoyable. Noticing what ignites a spark of interest in your child, then building on that will help enormously in encouraging them to develop perseverance, and take a delight in problem solving.

Enjoy the Simple Things
As with nurturing the *enterprising* element in your child, the emphasis is very much on enjoying the simple things, spending time together in a natural way, and recognising the 'teachable' moments when they arise, noticing

how your child responds with laughter, smiles, or a deep curiosity and desire to learn or experiment more.

It is also about noticing if things stop being fun for them or they are losing their sense of control over what counts as play, which can potentially inhibit their learning and enjoyment.

Enjoy the Here and Now

Being 'present' with your child during playtime, being attentive and aware of how they are playing, isn't just beneficial to your child but can provide a welcome relief away from all the day-to-day worries and concerns often on our minds. Being with your child in the 'here and now' also allows them to set the pace of their learning and play. Try not to worry about the mess that's being made and who is going to clear it up afterwards (maybe that could be a game too?), and pop your phone away to avoid the distraction of alerts, or thoughts about an email you should have sent. Just for this play time, enjoy the here and now and remember how it feels to really enjoy play.

Summary

These are some of the important aspects of Enjoyment:

- Enjoyment is the essence of Play, and all learning and development starts with Play.

- Play can increase and/or reinforce the bonds within your family.

- Enjoyment covers a wide spectrum – a balance is good between simple and relatively passive or contemplative moments of enjoyment, more organised or purposeful play, and moments of excitement and abandon.

- Play is a way to be with your child in the here and now, to put aside adult concerns and deepen the level of engagement experienced with your child.

- Enjoyment can occur in the everyday, it need not require special organisation or trips out.

Bringing the Three Es Together

The key to nurturing the character traits of can-do children of all ages lies in bringing together the Three Es. When they all come in to play, the magic happens.

Success in nurturing a Can-Do Child begins with effective *engagement.* You engage most effectively with your child using everyday playful situations and enjoyable activities, entering their world with acceptance and enthusiasm, amplifying and clarifying their experiences through questioning and mirroring, reinforcing your child's *enjoyment* of their relationship with you and in their own play and discovery. This provides the base upon which their innate *enterprise* and desire to act upon the world and learn from it can flourish and grow.

Playful activity is fun and engaging, enriching relationships between players. Mistakes are welcomed and when the pressure to perform or succeed is replaced with play and exploration for its own sake then having fun and making mistakes are just part of the learning process. This also creates a positive shared experience between players that reinforces the enjoyment and strengthens the relationship.

Using the Three Es approach at home underpins the acquisition of key cognitive skills and knowledge at school, with an emphasis upon overall character development and the ability to innovate and learn. It empowers parents, and encourages closer working between schools and families with a child-centred common vocabulary and framework.

From experience I have found that, as illustrated by the examples and activities presented in this book, the key to making this happen lies often in the everyday – recognising opportunities to bring all three elements together and to enjoy the experiences with your child.

Let the magic begin!

ACTIVITIES

"It was really affirming for me to see that I was already doing some of the suggested activities with my kids, and I understand better now how those are supporting the development of their can-do attitude and reaching their potential."

Richard Baldock, parent

"Children don't come with a manual so the best way I have of supporting parents is to give them a toolbox and allow them to choose the right tools at the right time. For me, the way The Can-Do Child is being delivered provides parents with some really cool tools for their toolbox."

Dr Amanda Gummer, UK's leading expert on play, play development, and child development

Introducing the Activities

The activities which follow illustrate the kind of fun you can have with your child in nurturing their can-do attitude, bringing together the three core elements of engagement, enterprise, and enjoyment. Whilst they take into account general developmental milestones, please note that recommended ages are intended as guidance only. It is important your child sets the pace at which they learn and that their innate curiosity to find out more takes precedence over rigid conceptions of age appropriateness.

Whatever their stage of development, or individual abilities, accepting that all children are different, it is important that your child's desire to know more is supported, so put aside anxieties about where you think they should be on the developmental path, as this will inevitably create stress for you and your child and inhibit their learning.

Finding the style of language and interaction to suit your own situation and child is really important. There is no prescribed way of carrying out the activities – you know your child better than anyone, and each family will have its own way of communicating and playing together. Do what feels right. I know of families who have a dedicated tech-free hour each day where family conversation is the priority, and those who aim to spend at least two hours of walking time together each week where many of my suggested activities come in handy. Meal times, bed times, holidays, car journeys, or simply standing in a queue – you will find as you become more familiar with the can-do philosophy and approach that the opportunities to introduce activities will naturally present themselves.

The sample activities provided here show how easy it is to nurture your Can-Do Child through everyday situations you find yourself in as part of family life. Whether that's waiting in a queue, on a long journey, at mealtimes, at the supermarket, or stuck inside on a rainy day. There is something for every situation!

Against each activity you will find a suggested starting age for the child, but do bear in mind what has already been said about not interpreting this too rigidly.

Similarly, it is indicated whether the activity is best suited to being at home or out and about, or indeed being done with others – in most cases the activities can work well with one or more children wherever you are (many require little or no resources other than imagination), so don't feel restricted by this.

At the end of each activity, you will clearly see the can-do characteristics and skills your child is developing and learning.

The activities are designed to be easy and fun, to happen in a natural way. Do work with your own intuitions and experience of what is best for your child at that moment in their development, and follow their pace. If a particular activity feels 'forced' and not naturally enjoyable, then trust your instincts to adapt and re-invent. The goal here is to support self-confident parents in raising happy, creative, confident children. This process starts with having faith in yourself and your child as you learn and grow through playing together.

Picture My Day

Often asking children to tell us about their day will elicit limited responses. Some may find it easier to draw a picture of their day instead but it can be difficult when faced with a 'blank canvas'.

Take a sheet of A4 paper (or A3 if you're feeling ambitious) and draw a line horizontally or vertically to separate yours and your child's day. You start by drawing something about your day in your space, then encourage your child to draw something about their day in their space.

You may well find your child naturally starts talking about what they're drawing anyway, but if not, spend some time reflecting on your respective pictures.

3+ YEARS

AT HOME

This is a relaxed activity, helping young children think about the act of remembering and then sharing information. Using pictures to portray events can be a valuable way of helping children develop vocabulary to talk about events and feelings as well as objects and facts, and is especially helpful with children who may yet lack the words to describe what they feel and perceive.

Creative and Innovative	Independent/ Self-Reliance	Imaginative
Resourceful	Resilience	Sound Judgements/ Decision-making
Self-Confidence	Adventurous	Curiosity
Social Skills	Ambition	Self-Regulation
Determination	Play and Work well with others	Social Awareness
Critical Thinking	Problem Solving	Planning and Organisation

Party Party

Children usually love a party, so why not encourage them to organise one at home – for the immediate family. They can decide whether to hold it inside or outside, have a small budget to purchase balloons or party poppers, make up notices and invitations, plan the music and any games, even have a few nibbles and soft drinks. It sounds a lot to organise but let them take the lead and be around to offer support if needed.

Planning a party at home provides a great opportunity for your child to develop their decision making, planning and organisation skills, and possibly some negotiation skills too. Have fun!

"I let my four-year old completely plan our family Boxing Day from deciding the menu to sorting out games and even the dress code. I was amazed with her ideas and her ability to plan and make lists (she sees me making to-do lists all the time!)"

Trusha, Mum and blogger at Secret StyleFile.com

Creative and Innovative	Independent/ Self-Reliance	Imaginative
Resourceful	Resilience	Sound Judgements/ Decision-making
Self-Confidence	Adventurous	Curiosity
Social Skills	Ambition	Self-Regulation
Determination	Play and Work well with others	Social Awareness
Critical Thinking	Problem Solving	Planning and Organisation

5+ YEARS

AT HOME

We're going on a family trip

Next time you're going out on a trip together, get your child involved in planning it. Once you've agreed where you're going and what you're doing, work with them to make decisions and get things ready: What's going in the packed lunch? What clothes to wear or take? They could even get involved in planning the route.

Help your child make a list which they can then put in order and allocate tasks to particular members of the family, including themselves. The list can be as long or as short as your child is happy with, ranging from what needs to happen before you leave e.g. feed the dog, close the windows, to responsibilities during the journey, on the activity, and even on return – for example who will be cleaning the muddy boots?!

Creative and Innovative	Independent/ Self-Reliance	Imaginative	**3+** YEARS
Resourceful	Resilience	Sound Judgements/ Decision-making	OUT & ABOUT
Self-Confidence	Adventurous	Curiosity	WITH OTHERS
Social Skills	Ambition	Self-Regulation	
Determination	Play and Work well with others	Social Awareness	
Critical Thinking	Problem Solving	Planning and Organisation	

5+
YEARS

AT
HOME

OUT &
ABOUT

WITH
OTHERS

We can work it out

Sibling play is probably one of the most common times for conflict at home either with siblings or visiting children. When things get too much it's often easier to seek a quick resolution to the conflict without involving the children: "You go and play in the lounge and George can play at the kitchen table." The issue with this approach is that it doesn't involve and engage the children in negotiating through the conflict so they are not learning crucial key skills such as listening, negotiating, and respecting differences.

"Conflict in the school playground is almost a daily occurrence, especially at this age. We believe it's important that children are involved in finding solutions to the problem so if, for example, one child has hurt another in the playground and they're both upset, we would encourage them to find a space (within sight) for 'quiet time' where they sit together and talk it out. They come back to us when they have sorted the problem."

Danielle Ellis, primary school teacher

There's no reason why this collaborative approach to resolving conflict can't be taken at home too, where the children are encouraged to come up with solutions to the problem, to try and resolve the conflict, which may of course include an element of compromise. Try sitting down with them to start and note some of the ideas they come up with, which can then be discussed, hopefully aiding a compromise/consensus to be reached.

5+ YEARS

AT HOME

OUT & ABOUT

WITH OTHERS

Creative and Innovative	Independent/ Self-Reliance	Imaginative
Resourceful	Resilience	Sound Judgements/ Decision-making
Self-Confidence	Adventurous	Curiosity
Social Skills	Ambition	Self-Regulation
Determination	Play and Work well with others	Social Awareness
Critical Thinking	Problem Solving	Planning and Organisation

Thinking about others

Involve your child when you help others – perhaps supporting an elderly neighbour or relative to cook a meal or take the rubbish out, or helping a local charity fundraise. Involving your child in these kinds of activities demonstrates and helps them practice kindness and empathy. To fully develop those traits, however, children need to be encouraged to think about others and there are a number of ways you can help with this.

Firstly as above, you can model it by taking action, or by verbalising thoughts such as "I wonder how Mrs Jones is feeling today" or "How do you think Mary felt when she fell over and hurt her knee?" Demonstrating kindness and consideration within family life or by showing empathy towards your child e.g. "I expect you feel cross about that" all helps your child learn these important qualities.

You can also help your child think about the feelings of others by engaging them in conversation about the experience of other people as well as their own emotional experiences.

3+ YEARS

AT HOME

OUT & ABOUT

Creative and Innovative	Independent/ Self-Reliance	Imaginative
Resourceful	Resilience	Sound Judgements/ Decision-making
Self-Confidence	Adventurous	Curiosity
Social Skills	Ambition	Self-Regulation
Determination	Play and Work well with others	Social Awareness
Critical Thinking	Problem Solving	Planning and Organisation

What's that worth then?

Around the age of five or six, children like to start helping out a little more around the house, for example sorting the washing, or setting the table for tea. This is an ideal time to begin teaching them about the relationship between work and money if you decide you're going to pay them for helping with certain tasks. Don't be surprised, though, if they start to try to negotiate on the value of tasks, particularly if you are also teaching them about saving and they have a target in mind.

It is important, even at this young age, to help your child begin to understand that not everyone has the same amount of money (or physical health, ability or shelter), so helping out should not always involve financial reward. It can be difficult for young children to understand the wider world context so one approach might be to buy something with the money they would have earned from, say, washing the car, to give to a charity. Discuss with them different types of charities and let them choose which one they would like to donate to. Tangible donations other than cash may help them understand the concept of social giving much better.

5+ YEARS

AT HOME

A cautionary note that almost certainly goes without saying: never let education about money get in the way of the most important lesson of all: that love is unconditional and comes without a price-tag!

Creative and Innovative	Independent/ Self-Reliance	Imaginative
Resourceful	Resilience	Sound Judgements/ Decision-making
Self-Confidence	Adventurous	Curiosity
Social Skills	Ambition	Self-Regulation
Determination	Play and Work well with others	Social Awareness
Critical Thinking	Problem Solving	Planning and Organisation

Role Play

"Dylan dressed up in his best clothes and took great pride in showing me around our house... They both love to role play and each time they do they are developing an awareness about, and their own understanding of, different jobs in society."

Claire M. Mum to Dylan (5) and Lloyd (2)

Role play is very popular with children and great for stimulating imagination and social interaction. There are so many possibilities with role play at home, from gardening centres (use plant pots, seed packets) to furniture shops; from estate agents to clothes shops and cafes (cold drinks, cakes). Let your child's imagination have free play, and encourage changing of roles between shopkeeper and customer.

If you have more than one child, get them all involved, and where, for example, they are setting up a café making drinks, encourage them to learn how to work together to get things done – taking and making up the orders, washing up etc.

3+ YEARS

AT HOME

This activity can be extended by following up on a home shopping delivery or shopping trip, using items from either. Encourage your child to help you make decisions about what to buy, through describing items in terms of their benefits (e.g. this sofa is so comfy; it will look perfect next to your chair) rather than features.

Creative and Innovative	Independent/ Self-Reliance	Imaginative
Resourceful	Resilience	Sound Judgements/ Decision-making
Self-Confidence	Adventurous	Curiosity
Social Skills	Ambition	Self-Regulation
Determination	Play and Work well with others	Social Awareness
Critical Thinking	Problem Solving	Planning and Organisation

If it can't be fixed…

It's a fact that at some point in the life span of children's toys, breakdowns happen. If it looks terminal, you could throw it out with the rubbish or at best attempt to recycle.

An alternative option is to open it up and explore. There may not be much to see, and of course caution is required, but giving your child the opportunity to look inside the toy, view the component parts, and get an idea about how it worked will stimulate their interest in understanding how things are made and may even inspire them to see if it can, after all, be fixed or perhaps even create a new object from the parts.

Emily Cummins, a young British inventor recalls spending many hours with her granddad helping him to make and fix things.

"At such a young age I was able to experiment and explore, he ignited my creative spark which is something I will always carry with me."

Emily age 4, in her grandad's shed.
Reproduced with kind permission from Emily Cummins.

Creative and Innovative	Independent/ Self-Reliance	Imaginative
Resourceful	Resilience	Sound Judgements/ Decision-making
Self-Confidence	Adventurous	Curiosity
Social Skills	Ambition	Self-Regulation
Determination	Play and Work well with others	Social Awareness
Critical Thinking	Problem Solving	Planning and Organisation

The Values Jar

This activity is based on 'The Key Jar' to stimulate conversation between family members and help develop a better understanding of each other.

On separate pieces of paper, write down lots of different scenarios or questions you can think of relating to social values that your child will understand or at least be able to have a go at answering and discuss with you. Here are some examples:

- If you were a superhero what would you change in the world?

- If you were given £2 too much change in a shop, would you let the cashier know?

- What would be the hardest thing about not being able to hear/being blind/being in a wheelchair?

- If you could do a good deed anywhere in the world, what would you do and where?

- Is it better to have too much of something or not enough of something?

Fold each piece of paper and place them in a jar. Over mealtimes or whenever the family is together and the time feels right, bring the jar out. Each family member takes a slip of paper from the jar, reads out their scenario or question and gives their response followed by a supportive discussion of the issue.

The values jar encourages children to try to articulate their opinions and reasons, and take different perspectives on situations. This can be modeled by other members of the family who answer the question they have chosen. Through discussion you can help them think through scenarios and how they feel. They will have the opportunity to reflect on moral and social values, and learn about values such as respect, responsibility, and honesty.

Creative and Innovative	Independent/ Self-Reliance	Imaginative
Resourceful	Resilience	Sound Judgements/ Decision-making
Self-Confidence	Adventurous	Curiosity
Social Skills	Ambition	Self-Regulation
Determination	Play and Work well with others	Social Awareness
Critical Thinking	Problem Solving	Planning and Organisation

Which Way to Go?

This is great activity which includes a strong element of chance but could well lead to some interesting discoveries when out for a walk! Take one ordinary dice and agree with your child a direction or instruction for each side of the dice, which you will need to follow when outside. For example, one dot would require you to walk straight ahead, two dots mean you turn left, three dots gives your child the opportunity to choose where you go next and so on. The possibilities for the kind of directions and/or instructions given are limited only by imagination and of course the physical walk you are on (make sure there are plenty of 'crossroads' or paths to make it more interesting but also be sure that it is an area you know reasonably well to avoid becoming completely lost!).

Write the instructions/directions down and take them plus the dice with you on your walk. Throw the dice whenever you reach a decision point e.g. pathway and if you can, follow the instruction. If it is simply not possible, keep throwing the dice until it lands on a direction or instruction which can be carried out, then continue.

5+ YEARS

OUT & ABOUT

WITH OTHERS

This activity is particularly challenging for children (and indeed adults) who struggle with uncertainty. It is a great way of learning to relax and discover the wonder of being adventurous – who knows where it may lead?

Creative and Innovative	Independent/ Self-Reliance	Imaginative
Resourceful	Resilience	Sound Judgements/ Decision-making
Self-Confidence	Adventurous	Curiosity
Social Skills	Ambition	Self-Regulation
Determination	Play and Work well with others	Social Awareness
Critical Thinking	Problem Solving	Planning and Organisation

7+
YEARS

OUT &
ABOUT

WITH
OTHERS

Geocaching

This variation of traditional hide and seek is fun, active, and teaches your child valuable team playing skills at the same time. Geocaching is a real outdoor treasure hunt game where players try to locate hidden containers (called caches) at various locations, using GPS-enabled devices.

Simply register at the web site,[10] enter your post code for the nearest cache then download the co-ordinates to your smartphone or GPS enabled device. Depending on where the cache is located, you can play this game on foot, by car or on bicycles.

Geocaching involves you all working together as a team – reading (indeed deciphering) the map co-ordinates and translating them into appropriate routes, finding each clue, inevitably getting lost and trying to find the correct route again. It is great fun and teaches the valuable lesson that effective communication between team members is vital for success. Your child

_____
10 www.geocaching.com

is also learning that everyone has strengths and weaknesses, but the success of a team is dependent upon everyone playing to their strengths.

Creative and Innovative	Independent/ Self-Reliance	Imaginative
Resourceful	Resilience	Sound Judgements/ Decision-making
Self-Confidence	Adventurous	Curiosity
Social Skills	Ambition	Self-Regulation
Determination	Play and Work well with others	Social Awareness
Critical Thinking	Problem Solving	Planning and Organisation

If I were in charge

Being a small child can be a frustrating experience, especially if you rarely get to call the shots! Most children can identify with the idea of being King or Queen, and having been exposed more to fairy tales than constitutional law they are unlikely at this age to believe that a monarch's rule is anything but absolute.

The question "What laws would you pass if you were king/queen?" opens up to your child a chance to dream, and to explore the implications of their dreams. The idea is not to encourage rampant megalomania but allow your child to give shape to their dreams, and in the process begin to reflect upon what would constitute a good life for them and for others.

Encourage them not to just stop at "Children could eat as many sweets as they wanted" and to explore their innate sense of what is fair and desirable. The underlying message should be that dreams are worthwhile in setting goals, and that the future is not fixed but is ultimately shaped in large part by our dreams and ambitions – you can easily point to many examples of advances in modern life that would have seemed like a crazy dream to people in the past.

"I take time to talk and explore everyday issues with Evan and Xander such as why customer service may have been poor or why food took too long to arrive. It's about exploring actions and consequences. Sometimes Xander will say 'I wish x would happen' and we talk about that, about why it might not happen."

Zoe Brown, Mum of five

Creative and Innovative	Independent/ Self-Reliance	Imaginative
Resourceful	Resilience	Sound Judgements/ Decision-making
Self-Confidence	Adventurous	Curiosity
Social Skills	Ambition	Self-Regulation
Determination	Play and Work well with others	Social Awareness
Critical Thinking	Problem Solving	Planning and Organisation

We're going on a poetry hunt!

Next time you're out walking with your child, whether on the way to school, in the park or on a woodland walk, use the sights and sounds to create some poetry together. Start off with the first line yourself and encourage your child to look around and come up with the next line of the poem. Take note of colours, smells, noises or even silence if you're lucky!

This activity is a great way for your child to get in touch with, and express thoughts and feelings about, their natural environment. Remember that poetry doesn't always have to rhyme – free verse poetry can be a wonderful way for your child to articulate what they see around them without having to worry about what rhymes with the last word in your line.

3+
YEARS

OUT &
ABOUT

WITH
OTHERS

Creative and Innovative	Independent/ Self-Reliance	Imaginative
Resourceful	Resilience	Sound Judgements/ Decision-making
Self-Confidence	Adventurous	Curiosity
Social Skills	Ambition	Self-Regulation
Determination	Play and Work well with others	Social Awareness
Critical Thinking	Problem Solving	Planning and Organisation

7+
YEARS

AT
HOME

OUT &
ABOUT

WITH
OTHERS

Tell me where to go

There are several ways to complete this activity depending on whether you'd like to be indoors or outdoors.

If indoors, have one child set up a simple obstacle course using whatever is available e.g. cushions. Another child is then blindfolded and has directions called out to them to lead them through the course.

If outdoors, then give directions to the person blindfolded to reach a particular destination, for example a park bench or a particular tree.

In either case, the person giving direction will need to speak clearly and ensure their instructions are understood. The person blindfolded will need to listen very carefully to carry out each instruction.

"You feel quite vulnerable because you haven't got your sight, and you rely on it so much and that's why it's so important that you listen to the other person. Ella really helped me near the end, telling me about my surroundings and directions. I thought she was really good."

Amy, age 12

For younger children, model this activity before they have a turn to ensure they know all the directions and location words necessary to give and follow each instruction. Key words they may need to include are: forwards, backwards, left, right, diagonal, to the left/to the right.

When the obstacle course is complete or they have reached the destination, remove the blindfold and talk about how easy or difficult it was to follow the instructions – what could have been improved or done differently? How well were the instructions followed? Learning how to give clear and concise information is an important skill, not only when completing academic work but also when expressing new ideas and thoughts. What's also really valuable in this activity is the whole process of imagining that you are someone else, thinking about the impact of your communications upon others and how things might seem to them.

Creative and Innovative	Independent/ Self-Reliance	Imaginative
Resourceful	Resilience	Sound Judgements/ Decision-making
Self-Confidence	Adventurous	Curiosity
Social Skills	Ambition	Self-Regulation
Determination	Play and Work well with others	Social Awareness
Critical Thinking	Problem Solving	Planning and Organisation

What if?

The "What if?" question is a really great one to help your child communicate their curiosity and creativity. It can lead to some very interesting discussions and insights into what your child is thinking. Developing the skill of critical thinking and articulating those thoughts takes time, but needn't be complicated.

For example, after watching a family movie, ask why they think a particular character behaved in a certain way, or how might they change the ending to make the film more happy/sad/ exciting.

Lots of fun can be had with story books by asking questions such as "How would the stories differ if Harry Potter or Alice in Wonderland were baddies?" Think of some really crazy questions such as: "What if... we had flying cars – would we need traffic lights and where would we put them?" How would we prevent mid-air collisions?"

Another way of asking is "Can you imagine?" an excellent prompt to encourage your child to think innovatively. Think about topics that interest your child and see what interesting questions you and your child can come up with. How about: "If you could build a robot, what tasks would you have it do? Would it be easier to build a robot that could open doors or a house that didn't have any?

This activity isn't about children coming up with the 'right' question, answer or solution, it's simply giving them an opportunity to try to articulate their thoughts and ideas, and develop their creativity or creative thought-process. This type of thinking and articulating takes time, so be patient. Try to model it yourself – talk out loud next time you're thinking a problem through.

Creative and Innovative	Independent/ Self-Reliance	Imaginative
Resourceful	Resilience	Sound Judgements/ Decision-making
Self-Confidence	Adventurous	Curiosity
Social Skills	Ambition	Self-Regulation
Determination	Play and Work well with others	Social Awareness
Critical Thinking	Problem Solving	Planning and Organisation

Pastime passions

Does your child enjoy tinkering or experimenting at home? This indicates an inquiring mind, and it's good to encourage them to learn a new skill, for example how to cook. Not only is this a practical skill, it can be thoroughly enjoyable and is the perfect outlet for experimenting with ingredients, flavours, or methods. You could have a budding chef who wants to apply scientific methods to cookery, just like Heston Blumenthal!

Jennifer Okpapi[11] fell in love with the ingredients and spices of her country of origin, Nigeria. From a young age, she loved to experiment in the kitchen, so her parents encouraged her by allowing her to cook for family mealtimes. As she became more proficient, her confidence grew, enabling her to experiment even further with different spices, ingredients and methods. Jennifer later managed to gain funding for her business and turned her passion for food into the UK's first cookery school dedicated to African cuisine. Her cookery school now offers a range of day classes as well as its own range of food products.

---

11 www.akhaya.com

If cooking isn't their thing, perhaps computers are? Encourage them to 'look under the bonnet' by exploring either the hardware (it is possible for you to build a PC with your child for instance; instruction books are available that will guide you through this process), or explore computer coding and programming. There are many opportunities for children to learn to code either through traditional class time or online.

Initially, carry out cookery or computer tasks together so they can watch how it is done, then allow them to continue by themselves. Resist the urge to watch over them, allow them to continue working unsupervised and encourage them to call upon you if they need help. Assure them that you know they will do an excellent job. At all ages children love to feel trusted and will enjoy being able to carry out an adult task all by themselves.

The motivation here is primarily intrinsic as you are building upon an interest that already exists. Do be careful to ensure that the task is age appropriate and matches their skill and ability, so that they are not overwhelmed by the task. When they are using or building upon a skill they already have, you will find your child is more likely to keep at it until the job is done and will be motivated to do the job well. They will have immense pride in their completed work.

Creative and Innovative	Independent/ Self-Reliance	Imaginative
Resourceful	Resilience	Sound Judgements/ Decision-making
Self-Confidence	Adventurous	Curiosity
Social Skills	Ambition	Self-Regulation
Determination	Play and Work well with others	Social Awareness
Critical Thinking	Problem Solving	Planning and Organisation

All together now

Putting on a family play, reading stories, or playing games together can enable your child to learn about the way in which tone and expression are varied to get particular messages across. Be as creative as you like and if, for example, you're reading a book together, work with your child to determine which kind of voices go with particular characters and why.

Creative and Innovative	Independent/ Self-Reliance	Imaginative
Resourceful	Resilience	Sound Judgements/ Decision-making
Self-Confidence	Adventurous	Curiosity
Social Skills	Ambition	Self-Regulation
Determination	Play and Work well with others	Social Awareness
Critical Thinking	Problem Solving	Planning and Organisation

7+ YEARS

OUT & ABOUT

Virtuous Challenge

This is an activity from our friends the Meek family, who in the Summer of 2014 sold their house, quit their jobs, and took Amy and Ella (then 11 and 8 years of age respectively) out of school to go on a year (and more as it turned out) of family Edventure.[12]

© Ross Grieve

If you've ever discovered money in your pocket you'd forgotten about, then it's always a pleasant surprise. This activity is simple to do yet guaranteed to put a smile on someone's face.

---

12 www.dotrythisathome.com

Whether at a camping, caravan, or youth hostel site, leave a small amount of money by the washing machine with a note to say 'Have a wash on us'.

7+ YEARS

OUT & ABOUT

Ella completed this challenge at the Brighton Caravan Club site. When reflecting on the challenge, she said: *"I would be amazed if I was going in the laundry and found a five pound note so I was excited when I did it. I drew some doodles on the note as well!"*

Creative and Innovative	Independent/ Self-Reliance	Imaginative
Resourceful	Resilience	Sound Judgements/ Decision-making
Self-Confidence	Adventurous	Curiosity
Social Skills	Ambition	Self-Regulation
Determination	Play and Work well with others	Social Awareness
Critical Thinking	Problem Solving	Planning and Organisation

Little Inventor

Introduce the idea of inventing by talking with your child about an invention they use regularly around the home such as the light switch or door handle. Now ask them to imagine they are an inventor. What would they invent? What problem would it solve?

Encourage them to talk about it, for example what would the invention be made of, or if they wish they can make some drawings. Depending on the complexity of what they've come up with they could even try making it.

The key is to engage their interest by letting them know you are genuinely interested in their ideas. Encourage them to put detail on their ideas and communicate their vision through thought-reflecting questions that encourage them to think things through without making them feel you are pouring cold water on it all. Remember, the goal at this age is to encourage communication, innovation, and creativity not to create a successful invention!

This activity can be expanded further to include your child finding out more about a particular invention, looking at how things are invented e.g. 'accidental' such as the Post-It note, and even looking at ways in which inventions could be improved upon further.

Creative and Innovative	Independent/ Self-Reliance	Imaginative
Resourceful	Resilience	Sound Judgements/ Decision-making
Self-Confidence	Adventurous	Curiosity
Social Skills	Ambition	Self-Regulation
Determination	Play and Work well with others	Social Awareness
Critical Thinking	Problem Solving	Planning and Organisation

Brighten my day

Curiosity in young children may range from the practical to the metaphysical. Encourage your child to think through solutions to everyday situations, for example how to brighten up the day when it's cold, wet, and wintry outside. Responses might include turning the heating up, wearing summer clothes, eating ice cream, or drawing pictures of a rainbow.

Creative and Innovative	Independent/ Self-Reliance	Imaginative
Resourceful	Resilience	Sound Judgements/ Decision-making
Self-Confidence	Adventurous	Curiosity
Social Skills	Ambition	Self-Regulation
Determination	Play and Work well with others	Social Awareness
Critical Thinking	Problem Solving	Planning and Organisation

Let them buy... dinner!

Liven up a trip to the supermarket by putting your child in charge of buying the dinner! Set appropriate parameters for them such as how much money they can spend, or whether there are particular foods that need to be included (or indeed excluded!). Agree the length of time they have to complete the shop and set them off. This takes a little bravery on your part, not least because you're likely to be the one having to cook it, but you may just be pleasantly surprised at the outcome.

After the shop, talk about what they found most challenging or easy, what they may like to do differently next time.

Creative and Innovative	Independent/ Self-Reliance	Imaginative
Resourceful	Resilience	Sound Judgements/ Decision-making
Self-Confidence	Adventurous	Curiosity
Social Skills	Ambition	Self-Regulation
Determination	Play and Work well with others	Social Awareness
Critical Thinking	Problem Solving	Planning and Organisation

Create your own currency

Long before money was developed, people used all kinds of possessions to trade for the things they wanted. There has been renewed interest in this over recent years where businesses 'barter' products or services of equal value without any physical cash changing hands.

Have your child devise their own form of currency they can use around the house – chocolate and sweets are likely to be the obvious first choices, however sparkly stones, marbles or buttons are more tooth-friendly alternatives. Help them assign 'values' to the currency and agree on what is to be 'traded' then see how they get on negotiating deals with you or other family members. For example, ask your child to collect 5 possessions that they feel have value or would interest other people. Next, arrange a trading time in which you all bring your goods; perhaps make it more formal by having drinks while you barter! You will probably need to lead the activity by explaining what you have, it's value, properties, and what you would like to exchange it for.

This is a fun activity for all. Deal making of any kind, whether with parents, friends, or in the world of work, will require your child to have great listening skills, to understand other's needs and the art of compromise, collaboration, and negotiation. All of these social skills take time to develop so be patient; even as adults we are challenged by daily situations which require the art of negotiation.

Creative and Innovative	Independent/ Self-Reliance	Imaginative
Resourceful	Resilience	Sound Judgements/ Decision-making
Self-Confidence	Adventurous	Curiosity
Social Skills	Ambition	Self-Regulation
Determination	Play and Work well with others	Social Awareness
Critical Thinking	Problem Solving	Planning and Organisation

Conversation starters

Conversation starters are a great way to engage your child in an easy, naturalistic way without the pressure of a series of questions.

Take a walk through the park or along the street – talk about what you can see, for example if you see a bird with a worm in its mouth, you might say "I've just spotted a bird that's caught a worm... I wonder if the bird is going to feed it to baby birds." Be careful not to use too much language so your child can contribute to the conversation. Pauses in your communication are a good way to slow down the pace of talking, so your child has thinking time. Remember conversations and chats should be a slow process – there's no need to rush.

It is good to encourage your child to talk by articulating observations that invite a response and perhaps generate questions. Children respond best when they believe you are really listening to them so "active listening" as opposed to a more distracted tone is appropriate. Put your mobile down, have eye contact, and encourage the conversation with non-verbal signals such as nodding, asking appropriate questions, and checking understanding by paraphrasing responses.

In a busy world it often feels easier to ask quick questions such as "What is that?" or "What did you do today?" to get a conversation started, however slowing down for a moment in the middle of your day and just commenting, creating no pressure on communication and saying to your child "tell me about it" can make a huge difference in children developing their ability to express themselves and to think more about their experiences and the world around them.

Creative and Innovative	Independent/ Self-Reliance	Imaginative
Resourceful	Resilience	Sound Judgements/ Decision-making
Self-Confidence	Adventurous	Curiosity
Social Skills	Ambition	Self-Regulation
Determination	Play and Work well with others	Social Awareness
Critical Thinking	Problem Solving	Planning and Organisation

i-Queue

Queuing is a fact of life in most countries, but the next time you're stuck in a queue with your child and tempted to check your watch, or sigh under your breath, have a chat with them about what they think could be done to make the queue move more quickly. Here's an example of how one Mum turned an unexpectedly long wait for food into an opportunity to do some problem-solving:

> *"On the way home from swimming with my 5 year old I stopped off at the drive-through. The queue of cars was unusually long and my son his usual hungry self. To pass the time, I asked why he thought it was so busy and whether he could think of anything that could be done to make the queue move faster. He gave some thoughtful responses wondering whether perhaps one of the food machines had broken down and commenting maybe there weren't enough staff."*

This kind of questioning and discussion not only helped to pass the time waiting in the queue, but also took the child's mind off his hunger, and encouraged him to come up with ideas, thinking about some of the processes involved for him to receive his food e.g. machines, and people. When he had talked about what may have happened to cause the queues he was then encouraged to think about possible solutions to the problem...

5+
YEARS

OUT &
ABOUT

> "...he said he thought there should be at least one person in the company who knew how to fix the machine if it had broken and that there should be a back-up one anyway. When I asked him about staff he replied 'there should be more', however when I explained maybe the company couldn't afford any more his response was 'well then they need to make the ones here smile more'. I'm guessing he was thinking that a smile goes a long way when people have been waiting a while – I couldn't argue with that!"

Creative and Innovative	Independent/ Self-Reliance	Imaginative
Resourceful	Resilience	Sound Judgements/ Decision-making
Self-Confidence	Adventurous	Curiosity
Social Skills	Ambition	Self-Regulation
Determination	Play and Work well with others	Social Awareness
Critical Thinking	Problem Solving	Planning and Organisation

How does your garden grow?

Whether you're fond of it or not, gardening can be a great way to show your child how from one tiny seed a whole plant, for example a tomato plant or sunflower, may grow. Try to find seeds of food your child or other members of the family may like then start the planting process. Encourage them to get stuck in to the compost and regularly look after the seedling by giving it water and plenty of light. They may like to measure the growth of the plant by using a height chart. The more involved they are in this the more they will understand the sequence of events required to create the vegetable they like. You can make this activity even more fun by helping them create weird and wonderful creatures or objects from their growing efforts such as a cress caterpillar or mini scarecrow.

Creative and Innovative	Independent/ Self-Reliance	Imaginative
Resourceful	Resilience	Sound Judgements/ Decision-making
Self-Confidence	Adventurous	Curiosity
Social Skills	Ambition	Self-Regulation
Determination	Play and Work well with others	Social Awareness
Critical Thinking	Problem Solving	Planning and Organisation

Jigsaw puzzles

3+ YEARS

AT HOME

WITH OTHERS

Chances are you will have a few jigsaw puzzles lying around the home. These are great little activities to help your child understand how piecing items together can make a whole. Resist the temptation to help them unless frustration sets in. If you don't have any jigsaws to hand try baking a tray of biscuit cake then using a range of different cutter shapes to see whether they can piece everything back together again. Or make your own simple jigsaws from pictures in magazines stuck to card and cut into shapes.

Creative and Innovative	Independent/ Self-Reliance	Imaginative
Resourceful	Resilience	Sound Judgements/ Decision-making
Self-Confidence	Adventurous	Curiosity
Social Skills	Ambition	Self-Regulation
Determination	Play and Work well with others	Social Awareness
Critical Thinking	Problem Solving	Planning and Organisation

Top Dog

In this activity, your child gets to be the boss! Very few children relish the idea of doing chores around the home, but this is a way to make them fun and encourages your child to take on more responsibility.

As boss they decide which chores need to be carried out, what equipment is required for each task and who carries out which particular chore. Give your child free reign and resist the urge to tell them what to do – discuss and plan together as a family instead.

The chances are your child will relish their new-found role as boss and simply delegate each task with glee. If there are siblings, there might be a squabble as to who does each job – highly likely in fact! How will they resolve this? Will they strike a bargain or use some crafty negotiation techniques? Are the tasks allocated appropriately so that they are achievable by, for example, younger siblings or less able members of the family? Are they showing consideration to others?

When the tasks have been completed, discuss who gets to be Top Dog next time round, and what lessons have been learned.

The idea is not to criticise anyone or to make comparisons, but simply to explore the way in which everyone has a role to play in working together, and leadership itself is more a matter of collaboration than hierarchy. An enterprising, Can-Do Child will learn to recognise the talents of others and motivate them to get involved. Learning to work with others effectively may be a life-long learning process, so your child needs all the support you can give them at this stage.

Creative and Innovative	Independent/ Self-Reliance	Imaginative
Resourceful	Resilience	Sound Judgements/ Decision-making
Self-Confidence	Adventurous	Curiosity
Social Skills	Ambition	Self-Regulation
Determination	Play and Work well with others	Social Awareness
Critical Thinking	Problem Solving	Planning and Organisation

Things To Do

You probably use a To Do list yourself and no doubt your child has seen you post this up somewhere like the fridge or computer. Encourage your child to set goals for themselves using the principle of a To Do list, but adapted to make it fun.

The idea is to make a list of things your child can accomplish by themselves. Depending on their ability, you can consider setting a time period – perhaps '7 things I would like to do in 21 days.' Explain that it is a good idea to set ourselves goals which are slightly challenging, as this helps us improve. Talk about things you always wanted to do as a child and, with help, managed to get done. Alternatively, if there was something you always wanted to do as a child, but never got round to accomplishing, discuss that too. Maybe this is the time for you to try!

If you are agreeing a time limit, your child might initially suggest unrealistic goals for the period, but this will still give you insights into what they want, what excites them or even what they fear. All of these provide clues about their motivation. What they would like to achieve could be made into a more suitable longer-term goal, in which case you could encourage them to think about intermediate steps or identifiable sub-goals.

The main thing is to work with what motivates your child, to encourage them to dream, but also to make their dreams realisable by identifying the route to success and setting markers along the way.

An example below is taken from a child's 14 day to-do list. Alex has Asperger's as well as mild co-ordination problems, so his original goals were amended to longer term goals, (those marked with an asterisk) and changed to the alternative 14 day challenge in brackets:

1. Overcome my fear of escalators* (go up the short escalators at the library once)
2. Write three different short stories – an adventure, a mystery and a comedy

3. Learn how to ride a bike* (steady myself twice, without falling off)

4. Make an Eiffel Tower structure out of Connex construction kit

5. Reach 50 kick-ups

Once your child has made their list, discuss the challenge together and decide if anything needs a plan of action to be drawn up, so that they know what steps they need to take. Be supportive throughout, offer advice with any items which your child might find particularly challenging and encourage them to stick with it. At the end of their challenge, make a big fuss of celebrating their success and then plan the next challenge.

Creative and Innovative	Independent/ Self-Reliance	Imaginative
Resourceful	Resilience	Sound Judgements/ Decision-making
Self-Confidence	Adventurous	Curiosity
Social Skills	Ambition	Self-Regulation
Determination	Play and Work well with others	Social Awareness
Critical Thinking	Problem Solving	Planning and Organisation

Ideas Diary

Encourage your child to keep an 'Ideas Diary' where they can make notes of interesting inventions they come across, questions about how things work, things they notice – which may include problems that need to be solved, interesting facts about nature or technology they observe, and of course ideas for inventions, drawings etc.

This may be one diary your child is happy to share with you, and it will provide you with some interesting insight into their developing, inventive mind.

Creative and Innovative	Independent/ Self-Reliance	Imaginative
Resourceful	Resilience	Sound Judgements/ Decision-making
Self-Confidence	Adventurous	Curiosity
Social Skills	Ambition	Self-Regulation
Determination	Play and Work well with others	Social Awareness
Critical Thinking	Problem Solving	Planning and Organisation

Amaze Me! / Amazing Me!

Depending on your child's interest and age, let them choose a selection of books or use the internet to discover more about amazing people who have made history. This could be anyone from William Shakespeare if they have a love of books, to Banksy or Picasso if they enjoy art.

Talk with your child about what these people have done, and what being 'amazing' might mean. Now ask them to think about people they've heard of or who they know, who they think are 'amazing' and create their own book cover or Wiki page equivalent about them.

Follow on with the 'Amazing Me!' activity to explore with your child what they think they might do in the future which is 'amazing'. What will people be saying about them? Encourage your child to put together a book cover or mock Wiki page about their future selves.

This activity will give you an interesting insight into how your child views themselves in the world, their dreams and desires and will naturally guide you in creating opportunities for them to follow their passions. A great example of this is Laura Tenison MBE, founder of JoJo Maman Bebe, interviewed for my first *Enterprising Child* book. She explained how as a child she discovered an interest in sewing. Her parents encouraged this interest by giving her a sewing machine as a birthday present and the fabrics she needed for her hobby.

Creative and Innovative	Independent/ Self-Reliance	Imaginative
Resourceful	Resilience	Sound Judgements/ Decision-making
Self-Confidence	Adventurous	Curiosity
Social Skills	Ambition	Self-Regulation
Determination	Play and Work well with others	Social Awareness
Critical Thinking	Problem Solving	Planning and Organisation

It's cash, but not as we know it

With contactless payment now mainstream, it's likely children are growing up rarely seeing and handling cash. When you're out and about with your child, try to make an effort to pay for transactions with cash and let them see and feel the actual money. If you're in a supermarket, let them help you use the self-service till, put the money in, and watch the screen as it is counted. In local shops, encourage your child to hand over the money to the shopkeeper and wait for the change and receipt. All these opportunities to handle money will help them understand that there are real constraints upon what is affordable based on what you actually have (in your purse, pocket, bank account), and avoid the infantile fantasy of unlimited wish-fulfilment that credit can encourage.

Creative and Innovative	Independent/ Self-Reliance	Imaginative
Resourceful	Resilience	Sound Judgements/ Decision-making
Self-Confidence	Adventurous	Curiosity
Social Skills	Ambition	Self-Regulation
Determination	Play and Work well with others	Social Awareness
Critical Thinking	Problem Solving	Planning and Organisation

Getting the measure of money

This activity involves playing a game to work out which type of money has the greatest value. For example, if your child held 10 lots of 10p pieces in one hand and a £5 note in the other, there's a good chance they will say the coins have more value simply because they are heavier. This is a good opportunity to discuss perceived as opposed to actual value, as you help them count the coins and perhaps begin to explore the ideas of trust and agreement that convey value upon bank notes and other types of 'paper money'.

Creative and Innovative	Independent/ Self-Reliance	Imaginative
Resourceful	Resilience	Sound Judgements/ Decision-making
Self-Confidence	Adventurous	Curiosity
Social Skills	Ambition	Self-Regulation
Determination	Play and Work well with others	Social Awareness
Critical Thinking	Problem Solving	Planning and Organisation

It's a goal!

Introducing the concept of saving money to your child plays an important part in helping them learn elements of financial responsibility. They don't need fancy piggy banks or toy cash machines; a simple clear jam jar can work just as well and allow your child to see the money being saved.

Patience can be a difficult lesson when children are young, so try to help them set small, achievable financial targets you feel appropriate for them, based on for example a new toy they would like or an activity they want to do such as a visit to the local adventure park. If your child is using a jam jar, have them make a label for it showing the target amount. Stay involved in the process, giving them praise for doing so well. Occasionally you may want to add to their savings with a little 'extra' to boost the funds giving them a surprise and some encouragement.

Once young children begin to understand the benefits of saving money, they are often keen to continue, so you can develop this understanding further as they grow, expanding to three jars – 'Save' 'Spend' and 'Share'.

Creative and Innovative	Independent/ Self-Reliance	Imaginative
Resourceful	Resilience	Sound Judgements/ Decision-making
Self-Confidence	Adventurous	Curiosity
Social Skills	Ambition	Self-Regulation
Determination	Play and Work well with others	Social Awareness
Critical Thinking	Problem Solving	Planning and Organisation

Move It! Mime It!

Choose a topic of interest to your child and encourage them to act it out with you through creative movements without speaking. For instance, if they are interested in Pirates you can mime scrubbing the ship's deck, looking out for other ships, searching for treasure on the beach, or fighting the enemy.

Put on some pirate style music in the background for added effect! Make the activity more engaging by turning this into a version of Charades. This is, however, much more than a good party game or an opportunity for some amateur dramatics of the silent movie variety;

learning to engage others and convey emotion without words, using facial expressions and body language, is an essential foundational skill.

Creative and Innovative	Independent/ Self-Reliance	Imaginative
Resourceful	Resilience	Sound Judgements/ Decision-making
Self-Confidence	Adventurous	Curiosity
Social Skills	Ambition	Self-Regulation
Determination	Play and Work well with others	Social Awareness
Critical Thinking	Problem Solving	Planning and Organisation

Coffee Cup Art

Next time you're going to a coffee shop, take some pens and pencils with you (some will supply these free of charge). Think of a relevant topic for your child/family and start decorating your cups – once they're empty of course!

© Priya Desai

Be inspired by the examples in the picture – 'Things I like' using the letters in your name, a cup from Pret inspired by their company wording, Halloween words, and as it was a Friday then activities for a Friday!

Get involved by working on your own cup and compare words and pictures with your child afterwards or take away the cup for your child to work on at home. What other creative ways of writing can you or your child come up with?

3+ YEARS

AT HOME

OUT & ABOUT

WITH OTHERS

Creative and Innovative	Independent/ Self-Reliance	Imaginative
Resourceful	Resilience	Sound Judgements/ Decision-making
Self-Confidence	Adventurous	Curiosity
Social Skills	Ambition	Self-Regulation
Determination	Play and Work well with others	Social Awareness
Critical Thinking	Problem Solving	Planning and Organisation

5+ YEARS

AT HOME

Giving back

Until now, you've probably sorted out your child's toys without their help, deciding whether to throw away, donate to charity or friends, or sell. Now they're just a little older, give your child the opportunity (Christmas and birthdays are good times) to sort out their toys and create different piles – one for charity, one for throwing away and so on. Explain to them the importance of keeping the *throw away* pile to a minimum – thinking environmentally, but also in value terms *one person's rubbish being another's treasure* – and help them work out what toys could be mended or cleaned and then be given to charity.

Building on this, have a look and see what local charities operate around say Christmas time to support struggling families or children in care. They will often put calls out for donations of clothes and toys for children so even if your child doesn't want to part with anything of theirs, you could go shopping with them so they may choose a toy or an item of clothing to donate. If this is a regular call-out for help from the charity, then link this activity up with *'It's a goal'* and encourage older children to set a target to reach which will enable them to buy a new toy for someone-else less fortunate.

Creative and Innovative	Independent/ Self-Reliance	Imaginative
Resourceful	Resilience	Sound Judgements/ Decision-making
Self-Confidence	Adventurous	Curiosity
Social Skills	Ambition	Self-Regulation
Determination	Play and Work well with others	Social Awareness
Critical Thinking	Problem Solving	Planning and Organisation

Look what I've learnt!

Reserve a physical space e.g. a board on a wall where your child can keep memories of exciting things that they have learnt. For children of school age, ask them to tell you one exciting/ interesting thing they have learnt during the day or week, and get them to write a short note about it to stick on the board. For younger children you could write it down as they speak or they can make a drawing and stick it to the board.

If your child has been with you during the day you will be able to remind them of the different things that happened, perhaps picking up leaflets or keeping tickets related to a fun activity you have done together. If they have been at school then useful questions may be *"what did you enjoy and like today?"* or *"tell me about something exciting you learnt at school today."*

What you are creating here is a wall of discovery – things which excite or interest your child – new pictures, facts, and ideas which ignite a spark in them. Having visuals and pictures as an inspiration, will naturally get your child talking about what they like and are interested in.

Creative and Innovative	Independent/ Self-Reliance	Imaginative
Resourceful	Resilience	Sound Judgements/ Decision-making
Self-Confidence	Adventurous	Curiosity
Social Skills	Ambition	Self-Regulation
Determination	Play and Work well with others	Social Awareness
Critical Thinking	Problem Solving	Planning and Organisation

Show it off

If you have a local show or community event taking place, find out whether there are categories young children can enter. If there are no categories for children, why not suggest to the organiser that children run an 'enterprise table' – this works well at Christmas time when children make up to say half a dozen items of their choosing (hama bead cards, jewellery, painted pebbles are just a few ideas!) which are then presented on the children's table for visitors to buy.

A local show can offer plenty of opportunities for children to get involved in activities such as cooking, painting or even making an animal out of vegetables! This will give your child a boost by just seeing their designs on the table ready for judging. They may not win a prize, but that is true in life generally – not everyone wins first prize, but the most important thing is they have tried (you can always make your own little rosette to give them for entering and don't forget to take a photograph of their entry on the table) and can learn from the other entries what they could do differently next time, as one

"When my son turned four he was old enough to enter the local Agricultural Society County Show. We looked through the categories and as he loved to bake he entered 'chocolate crispy cakes on a paper plate'. He also decided to enter a painting under the theme of 'Sunlight' and create a paper plate fish.

He was so excited taking the entries over before the show opened, it made him feel very important! We visited the show on the final day to discover he had won second prize for the crispy cakes and painting, and highly commended for the paper plate fish. What surprised me most was how much time he spent looking at the entries which won first prize. When I asked him why he was doing that he said 'so I can see why they're better than mine and I can win first prize next time."

Creative and Innovative	Independent/ Self-Reliance	Imaginative
Resourceful	Resilience	Sound Judgements/ Decision-making
Self-Confidence	Adventurous	Curiosity
Social Skills	Ambition	Self-Regulation
Determination	Play and Work well with others	Social Awareness
Critical Thinking	Problem Solving	Planning and Organisation

How will I know when it's working?

Two questions I am frequently asked are:

- How difficult is it for parents to implement the can-do philosophy and approach?

- How will I know when it's working?

I have stressed this is not a book or approach which places extra burdens upon parents, and equally no-one would ever wish to place these upon their children either, especially at a time when research suggests many are becoming increasingly stressed as already noted.[13] The beauty of the Can-Do Child approach is that we use play-centred, everyday situations and straightforward activities which are inherently enjoyable for all involved to help children do what comes naturally, which is to learn and develop through play and to explore and develop their own creativity, imagination, problem solving and interpersonal skills.

---

13 The Cambridge Primary Review Trust

These are activities and situations in which there is no pressure to succeed or get it right, this is learning through fun that leads to an increase in self-confidence and self-esteem, not an increase in tension and worry.

I know parents face many pressures upon their time, and children are becoming increasingly over-scheduled with extra-curricular/after-school actvities. However, I also know that even if they are unable to find more time, parents would like to increase the quality of the time that they do spend with their children. The can-do approach helps with this by providing easy and practical ideas for simple activities, in a context where children naturally succeed, experiencing the time together as being supportive, enjoyable, and interesting.

So, how will you know whether the can-do philosophy and approach you put into practice in your family is working? Well, over time you will see a difference in your child, with a noticeable increase in their creativity and independence of thought, increased self-confidence, increased ability to get along with others and communicate effectively, improved problem solving, tenacity, and self-discipline.

"It [The Can-Do Child] has given me ideas for how to lead their play in a way that stimulates their creative thinking and problem solving ability. I certainly feel like it is helping them develop into confident, independent children."

M Davidson, Dad to 9 year old and 5 year old

Whilst a Can-Do Child is a resourceful, happy, creative, confident one, it is important to remember that they are unlikely to be all of those things all of the time – we must accept that providing a secure base for them also means accepting that sometimes they will be sad or afraid, and just because they are generally happy, creative, and confident doesn't mean they will eat all their veggies, co-operate when you need it most, and be consistently kind and thoughtful. A Can-Do Child is still a child, and not a candidate for sainthood! This caveat aside, I am confident you will notice and appreciate the difference in your child as you implement the Three Es approach.

As well as observing the positive impact of your efforts upon your child, it is important to pay careful attention to the ways in which you find yourself becoming more creative and self-confident as a parent, noticing how the quality of your engagement with them becomes more a source of pleasure, and less perhaps an area of concern or worry. In keeping with the can-do philosophy, the goal is to help you and your child be yourselves, to own, celebrate, and nurture your unique, amazing potential and abilities, and of course to have fun together.

I sincerely hope this book will really help you enjoy the play times with your child, give you plenty of ideas to keep them busy, and inspire you to stay in touch with the enterprising, Can-Do Child within yourself. You are the most important person in your child's life, and as shown throughout this book, their future really does start with you.

A CAN-DO GENERATION: THE NEXT STEPS

Many parents are doing their very best to help support their child's creativity and zest for life, however there remains a general lack of focus on the role and significance of parents in nurturing children's character traits and skills which will help them not just enjoy the experience of childhood exploration and play, but give them that all important can-do attitude and approach to help them on their way, working towards fulfilling their full potential. Far too many parenting approaches are focused on simply modifying behaviour. My concern is for the building of overall human potential through the love and support children receive from their parents. My vision is that through the nurturing they receive from parents, carers, and educators using the can-do philosophy, methods and tools, children can be the creators of a better tomorrow. I hope that having read this book you will want to be a part of creating that better future too.

To supplement the work with parents we are also working with education and care providers to enable a more seamless and child-centred approach to integrating the philosophy and methods throughout curriculums, bridging the gap between school and home with an integrated framework of values and practical methods dedicated to the welfare of the child which enables them to realise their full potential.

Now you have read this book, you will have a good grasp of the way to use the Three Es model to nurture your Can-Do Child. However, I understand that parents need all the support and inspiration they can find.

Working with professionals from the fields of parenting, child psychology, early years, enterprise education, and activity based learning providers we have developed further resources to support you in helping your child develop their can-do approach to life. To learn more about all we have to offer in the way of support and help, and keep up to date with our latest work please visit www.candochild.com.

I hope you have found inspiration and practical support in this book and that you will join in and be a part of the Can-Do Child community as we continue to learn from each other, and from our children, about the ways in which we can support them to realise their potential, their hopes, and their dreams.

ACKNOWLEDGEMENTS

Through the course of writing this second book, I am reminded once more how generous others are with their time – telling their stories of childhood, parenting, and teaching, sharing experiences and their wisdom, for which I will always be indebted.

The Enterprising Child Advisory Board has played an important part in the development of the Can-Do Child philosophy, as well as providing wonderful support to me personally, so I would like to thank them individually as follows:

Sue Atkins
International parenting expert
Phil Benson
Entrepreneur, educator and speaker
Priya Desai
Speech and language therapist
and children's author
Dr Amanda Gummer
UK's leading specialist in play,
play development, and child development
Dipesh Patel
Global Analytics Director at Unilever

I would also like to acknowledge the following contributors and supporters:

Richard Baldock and family, Dr Teresa Belton, Jenny Briggs, Zoe Brown and family, Tanith Carey, Mary Cummings and family, Jasmine and Ben Cutting and family, M Davidson and family, Demos, Danielle Ellis, Caroline Hass, Jacqueline and Nicholas, Dr Lynne Kenney, Paul Lindley, Adam Matich, Tim, Kerry, Amy and Ella Meek, Claire Meredith and family, Beatriz Nasr and George, NCPFCE, Jennifer Okpapi, Cheryl Ryder and family, Monica M. Smith, Laura Tenison MBE, Trusha, my husband Chris for his generosity of time and ongoing support, and my son Dylan for showing me just what can-do really means in the everyday.

Thank you to Phil Taylor-Guck for his belief and investment in myself and the work of Enterprising Child.

Finally a huge thank you to my publisher Rethink Press for their skills and patience in guiding me through each stage to reach this final production.

THE AUTHOR

 Lorraine Allman is a writer, speaker, broadcaster, and educator with over 17 years' practical experience working on a wide range of projects involving young people, and small businesses.

Lorraine works with organisations both in the UK and abroad to develop toolkits and programmes for nurturing a can-do mind and skills set in young people. She has a long term commitment with the Women at Work Foundation, developing and rolling out an Enterprising and Life Skills programme for young learners in the township of Alexandra, South Africa.

She has collaborated with parenting, child development and early years experts in both the UK and US, with her work featured across newspapers, parenting and educational magazines, and digital platforms. She is a popular guest speaker on radio and at national events such as the Education Show.

Lorraine is an honorary member of, and expert adviser to, the Board of the National Early Years Trainers and Consultants Organisation (NEyTCO), judge for the Young Enterprise

Fiver competition in UK Primary Schools, and delivers inspirational workshops to schools and universities supporting the National Assembly for Wales's Youth Entrepreneurship Strategy.

Lorraine is passionate about supporting parents and educators to nurture Can-Do children, helping them grow up to be happy, confident individuals, achieving their full potential.

She lives in West Wales with her husband and 10-year-old son who is the UK's first young ambassador for Crowdfunding.

www.lorraineallman.com
https://uk.linkedin.com/in/lorraineallman
@beindemand

Lightning Source UK Ltd.
Milton Keynes UK
UKOW06f0734210117
292576UK00009B/114/P